Journey of a T-shirt

John Malam

www.raintreepublishers.co.uk
Visit our website to find out more information about Raintree books.

To order:
Phone 0845 6044371
Fax +44 (0) 1865 312263
Email myorders@raintreepublishers.co.uk

Customers from outside the UK please telephone +44 1865 312262

Raintree is an imprint of Capstone Global Library Limited, a company incorporated in England and Wales having its registered office at 7 Pilgrim Street, London, EC4V 6LB – Registered company number: 6695582

Edited by Dan Nunn and Diyan Leake
Designed by Cynthia Della-Rovere
Original illustrations © Capstone Global Library Ltd 2012
Illustrated by Capstone Global Library Ltd
Picture research by Mica Brancic
Production by Alison Parsons
Originated by Capstone Global Library Ltd
Printed and bound in China by Leo Paper Products Ltd

ISBN 978 1 406 23936 2 (hardback)
16 15 14 13 12
10 9 8 7 6 5 4 3 2 1

British Library Cataloguing in Publication Data
Malam, John, 1957–
Journey of a T-shirt.
687-dc22
A full catalogue record for this book is available from the British Library.

Acknowledgements
The author and publishers are grateful to the following for permission to reproduce copyright material: © 2010 Superstock p. 21; Alamy p. 22 (© Martin Jenkinson); Corbis pp. 8 (© Mark E. Gibson), 9 (© AgStock Images), 12 (© Sasha Woolley), 13 (© AgStock Images), 14 (© Yannick Tylle), 15 (Corbis/Dagens Naringsliv/ © Orjan F. Ellingvag), 17 (© moodboard), 26 (dpa/ © Frank May), 31 top (© AgStock Images), 31 middle (© Sasha Woolley); Getty Images p. 23 (© AFP Photo); iStockphoto.com pp. 18 (© sorendls), 19 (© Adam Korzekwa); Shirtworks.co.uk p. 24; Shutterstock pp. 1 (© Péter Gudella), 3 (© Péter Gudella), 4 (© Monkey Business Images), 5 (© Péter Gudella), 6 (© Walter G. Arce), 10 (© Danny E. Hooks), 11 (© RoxyFer), 25 (© Anyka), 27 (© Darrin Henry), 28 (© Darrin Henry), 29 top (© RoxyFer), 29 bottom (© Péter Gudella); Superstock pp. 16 (© giovanni mereghetti), 20, 31 bottom (© giovanni mereghetti).

Cover photographs of T-shirts on a clothesline (© Mike Flippo) and a cotton boll (© Heidi Brand) reproduced with permission of Shutterstock.

Every effort has been made to contact copyright holders of material reproduced in this book. Any omissions will be rectified in subsequent printings if notice is given to the publisher.

Contents

Some words are shown in bold, **like this**. You can find out what they mean by looking in the Glossary.

What will you wear today?

Pull on a T-shirt and you are ready for the day! T-shirts are such simple pieces of clothing. They come in lots of colours, and they look great, whether plain or with patterns on them.

Have you ever wondered why it's called a T-shirt? It's because it makes the shape of a letter T when it's flattened out. But how is a T-shirt made? Turn the page to find out.

Cotton for T-shirts

Most T-shirts are made from cloth called cotton. Cotton cloth comes from the cotton plant. Cotton grows in more than 100 countries around the world.

These cotton plants are growing in a farmer's field.

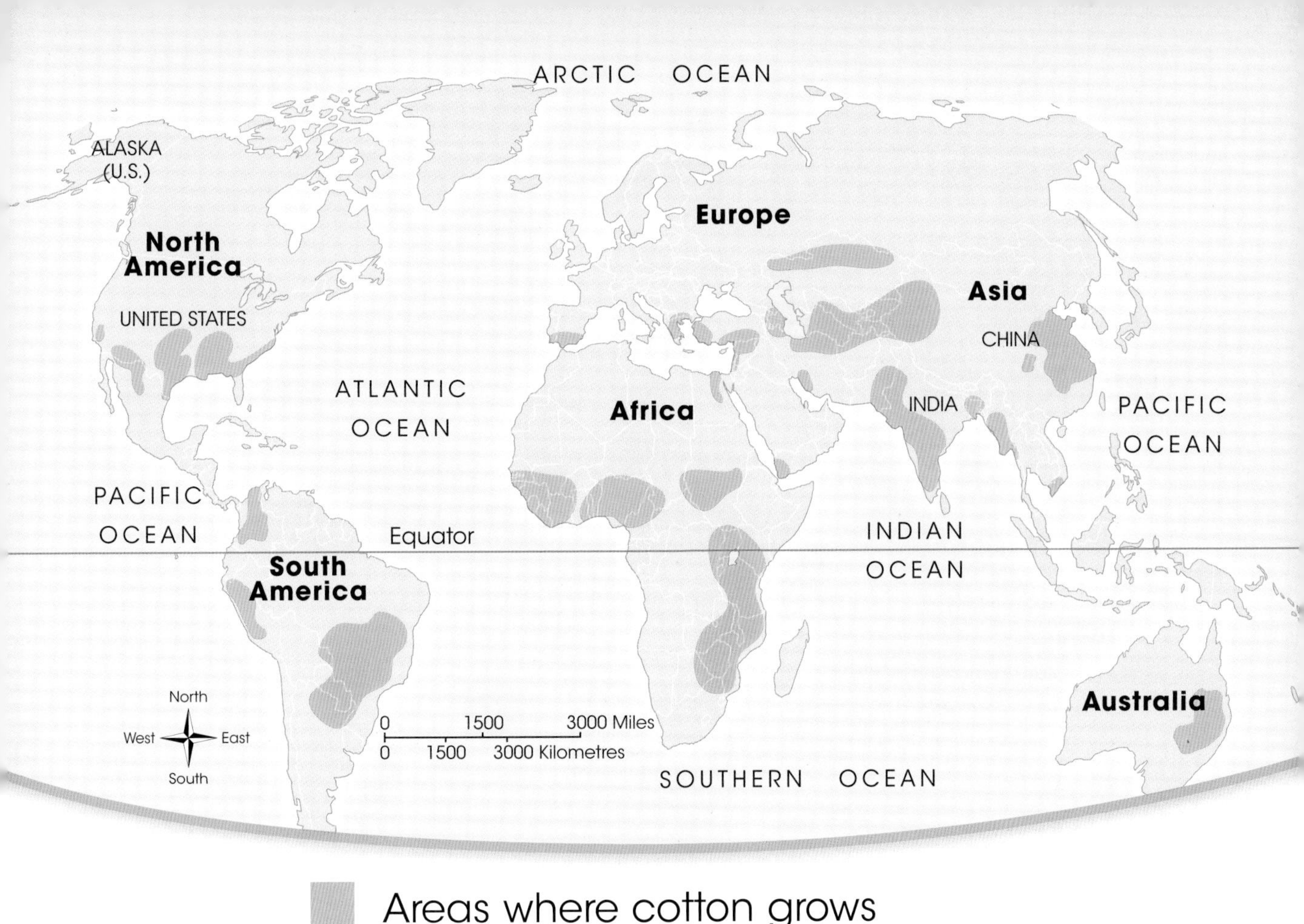

Cotton plants grow in warm, sunny places where there is a good amount of rain during the growing season. Most of the world's cotton is grown in China, India, and the United States. Cotton plants grow in the southern part of the United States.

Growing the cotton

Farmers in the United States **sow** their fields with cotton seeds between March and May. After a few days, **seedlings** appear. The cotton plants grow to about 1.2 metres (4 feet) high. They have flowers when they are three months old.

This is the flower of the cotton plant.

This is a cotton boll.

At first, the flowers are creamy white. Then they slowly change colour to red. After a few days, the flowers die. The dead flowers fall off the plants. There are small green pods left behind. They are called cotton **bolls**.

Inside a cotton boll

Each **boll** is full of seeds. Cotton **fibres** grow from the seeds. The boll gets bigger until it is about 3 centimetres (just over an inch) across. It **ripens** in the sun, turns from green to brown, and bursts open.

Cotton fibres burst out of the ripe bolls. There are about half a million fibres in every boll. They are white and fluffy.

Picking the cotton

In the United States, farmers **harvest** cotton between August and December. Machines move up and down the rows of cotton plants. They pick the fluffy white cotton **bolls**.

The bolls are squashed together inside the picking machine. They come out as **modules** of **seed cotton**. The modules look like giant loaves of white bread!

Making cotton lint

Farmers send the **modules** of **seed cotton** to a **factory**. The factory is called a cotton gin (say: jin). *Gin* comes from the word *engine*. At the factory, machines break open the modules. Cotton **fibres** spill out.

This machine is removing cotton fibres from the seeds.

The cotton seeds are still attached to the fibres. Machines separate the fibres from the seeds. The loose fibres are called cotton **lint**. They are pressed into big, heavy **bales**.

Combing the cotton

The **fibres** in cotton **lint** are tangled up. They criss-cross each other in all directions. To make the lint into cloth for T-shirts, the fibres must be straightened out. This is done at a **factory** where cotton cloth is made.

The lint goes into a carding machine. It combs the fibres over and over until they lie in straight lines. The machine turns the lint into a long, chunky rope of soft cotton. The rope is called a **sliver** (say: sly-ver).

Spinning and weaving

The next step is to spin the cotton **sliver** into cotton **yarn**. A spinning machine pulls a long line of **fibres** out of the sliver. It twists the fibres round and round.

The spinning machine twists the fibres tightly together to make yarn or thread.

To make cloth for T-shirts, the yarn is put on to a **loom**. The loom **weaves** the yarn into long lengths of cloth. It works with lots of rows of yarn at a time. The cloth is plain white.

White or coloured cloth?

If the cotton cloth is for white T-shirts, the cloth is **bleached** to make it bright white. If it is for colourful T-shirts, the cloth needs to be coloured with **dye**. It is put inside a machine that works like a giant washing machine.

Water and dye slosh around in the machine until the cloth has changed colour.

These rolls of finished cloth are ready to be laid out and cut.

The wet cloth is squeezed to get all the water out. Then it is dried and rolled up. It is ready to be made into T-shirts.

Making a T-shirt

The cloth is laid flat on a big table. There are lots of layers, one on top of another. Outlines of the T-shirt pieces are marked on the top layer. A cutting machine follows the outlines and cuts out the pieces.

This machine cuts through the layers of cloth.

A sewing machine stitches the pieces together. Front and back are joined at the sides to make the body. Then the sleeves are attached. Last of all, the collar is joined to the body.

Carried by ship

T-shirts are made in **factories** all over the world. They are folded and packed into cardboard boxes. The boxes hold lots of T-shirts.

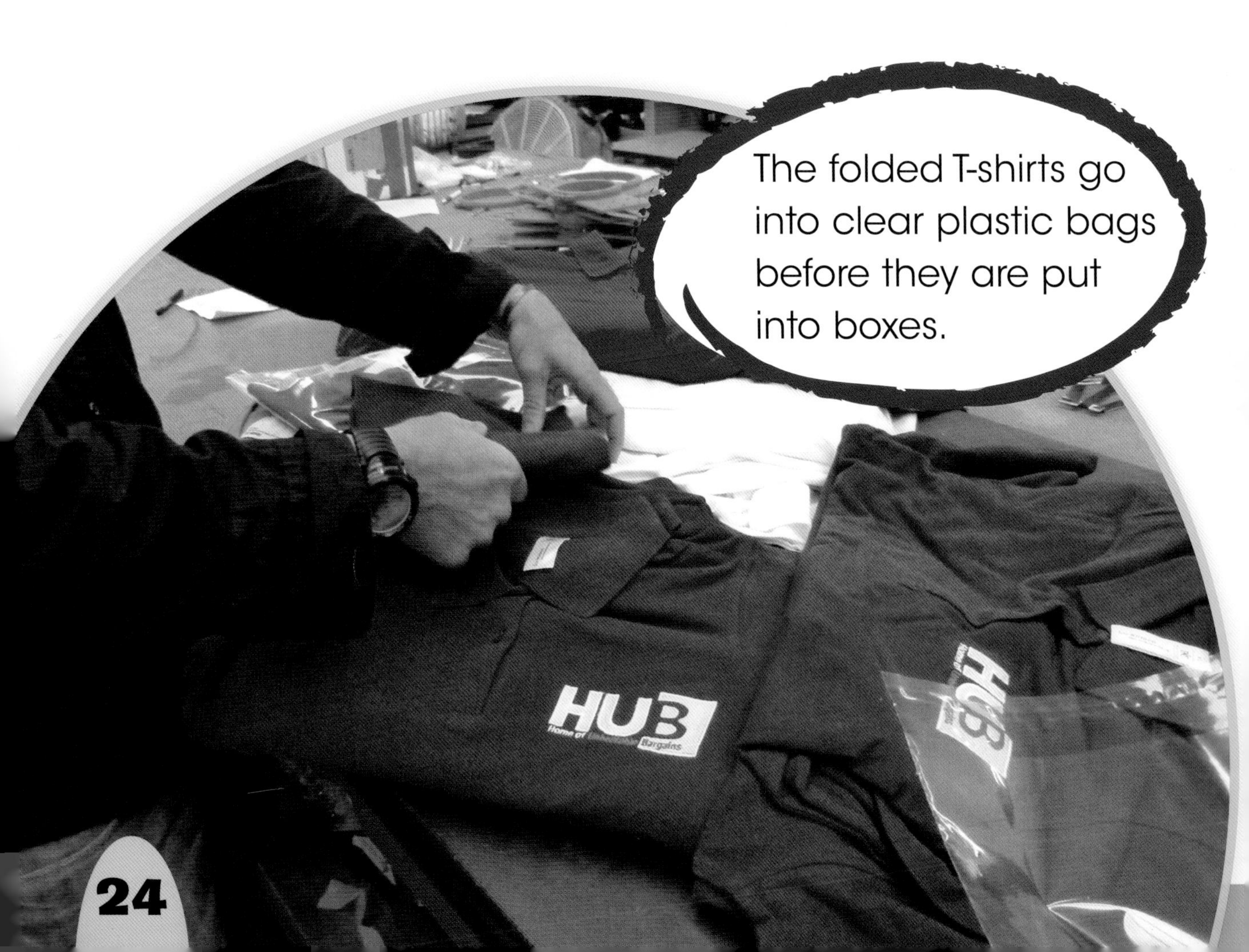

The folded T-shirts go into clear plastic bags before they are put into boxes.

If the T-shirts have been made in a faraway country, a **cargo ship** will carry them to where they are needed. They will travel inside big metal boxes called **containers**.

Into the shops

It might take a few weeks for the **cargo ship** to sail to your country. When it does, it unloads the **container** of T-shirts. Then the T-shirts are sent to shops.

The T-shirts are put on shelves in a shop.

People pay the shops for the T-shirts. In turn, the shops pay the **factory** that made the T-shirts. The T-shirt factory pays for the cotton cloth. The farmer who grew the cotton must also be paid.

Your new T-shirt

It takes about six months for cotton seeds to grow into plants with **ripe** cotton **bolls**. Then it can take another six months to turn the cotton into your lovely new T-shirt.

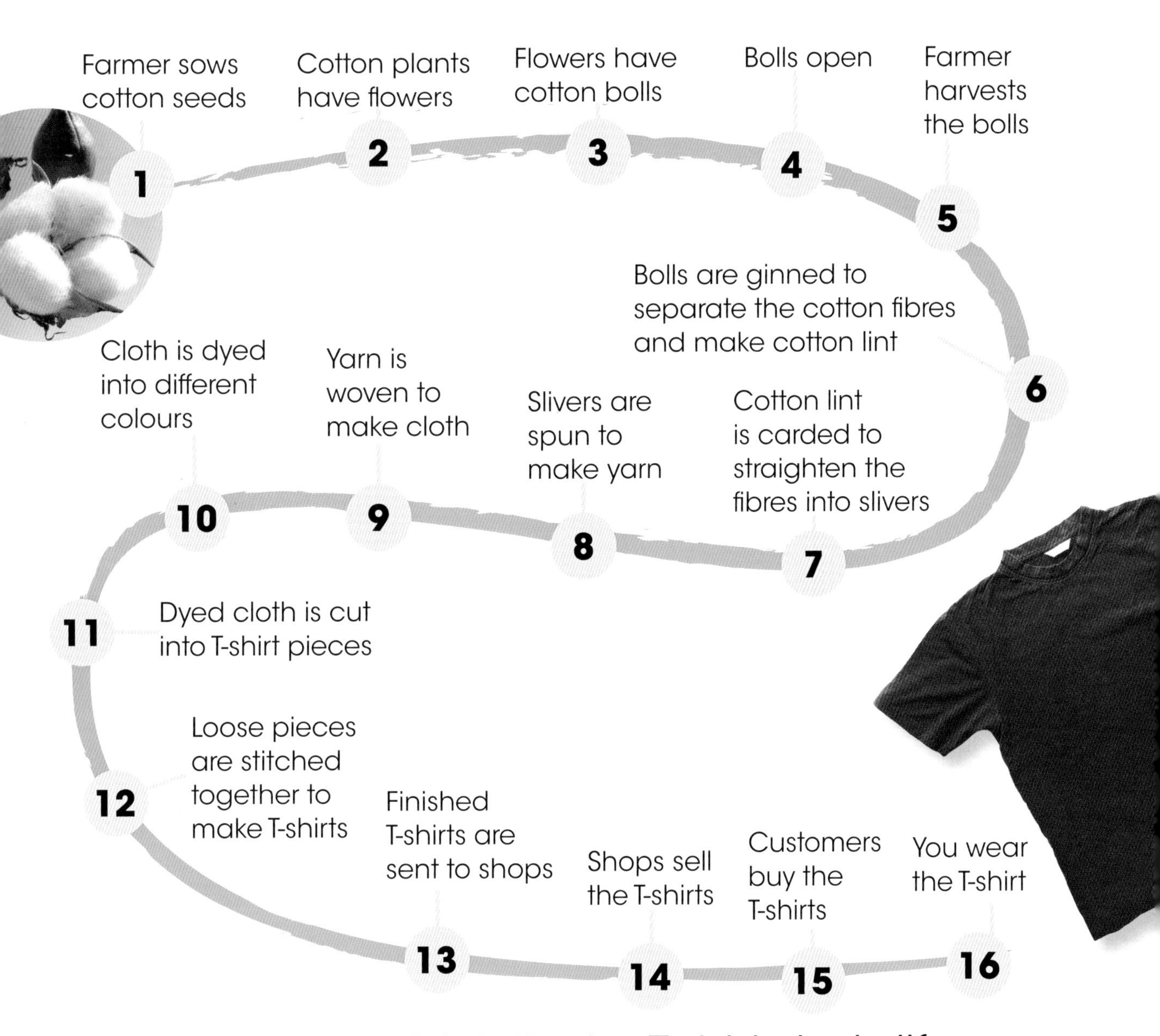

It's amazing to think that a T-shirt starts life as tiny seeds planted in a farmer's field somewhere in the world.

Glossary

bale cotton that has been pressed into a large bundle
bleach make something turn white
boll seed head of the cotton plant
cargo ship ship that carries goods (cargo)
container large metal box filled with cargo
dye substance used to change the colour of cloth
factory building where things are made
fibre thin strand of cotton that cloth is made from
harvest time when farmers gather in their crops
lint soft, fluffy material
loom machine for weaving yarn into cloth
module massive block of seed cotton that has just been picked
ripe fully grown and ready to pick
seed cotton raw cotton straight from the field
seedling baby plant
sliver rope of cotton made by a carding machine
sow plant a seed
weave form yarn into finished cloth
yarn cotton that has been spun into a fine thread

T-shirt quiz

1. What are most T-shirts made from? (see page 6)
2. What are the small green pods on cotton plants called? (see page 9)
3. When do farmers in the United States harvest their cotton? (see page 12)
4. What does a carding machine do? (see page 17)
5. What weaves the yarn into long lengths of cloth? (see page 19)

Find out more

Click on "The Many Faces of Cotton" link on this website to find the answers to many questions about cotton:

www.cotton.org/pubs/cottoncounts/resources.cfm

Find out about the history of cotton on this website:

www.historyforkids.org/learn/clothing/cotton.htm

Answers

1. cotton, 2. cotton bolls, 3. between August and December, 4. It combs the cotton to make the fibres straight, 5. a loom

Index